Nieuw Pfalz

Scale 280 Rods to the Inch

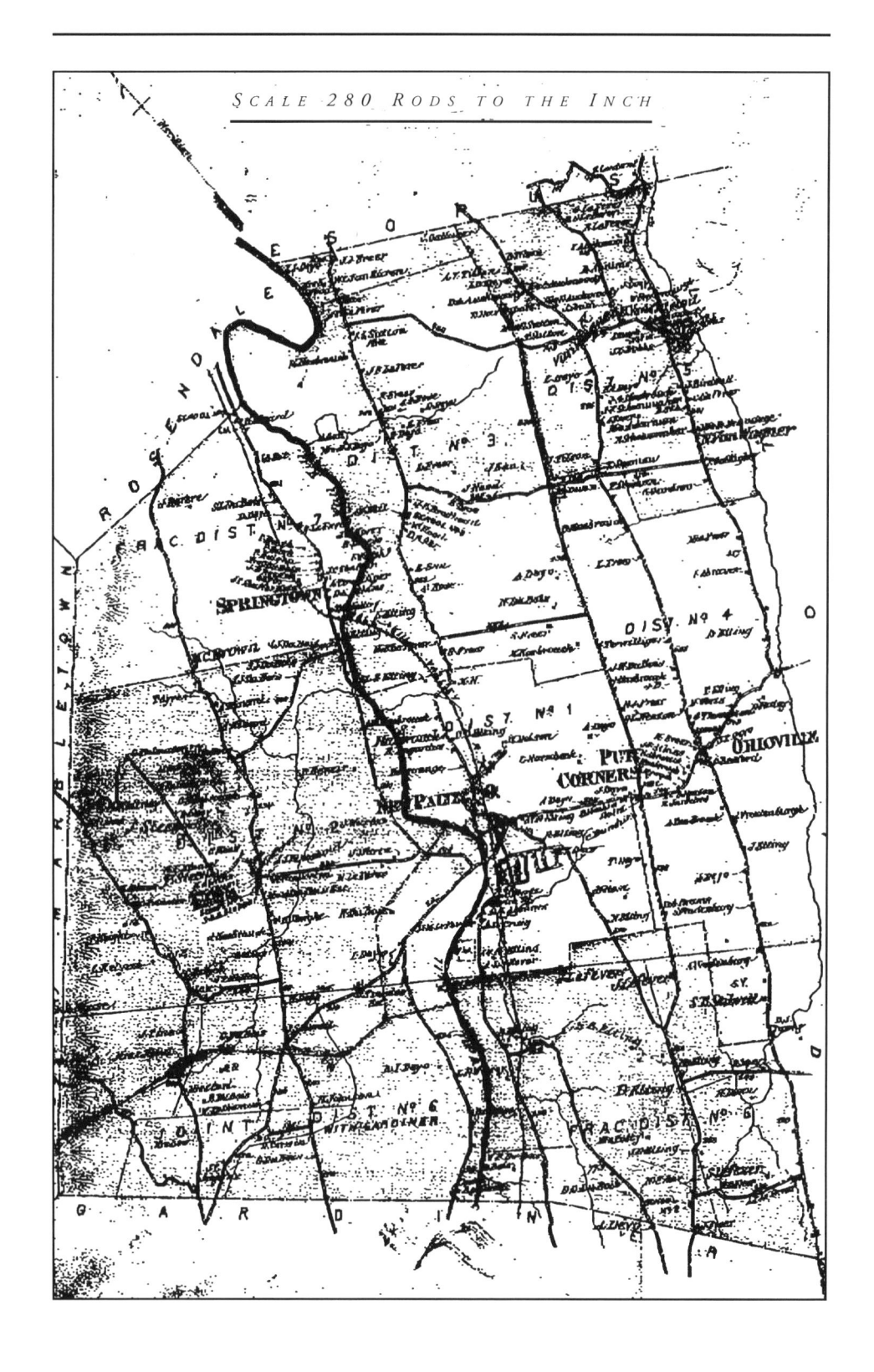

Nieuw Pfalz

BOOK 1

The Burial

A Poem by

David Appelbaum

Published by Codhill Press   New Paltz   New York

All rights reserved.

© 2004 David Appelbaum

ISBN 1-930337-14-0

Designed by Martin Moskof

Published by

Codhill Press

New York   New Paltz

www.codhill.com

Book 1

The Burial

Part 1

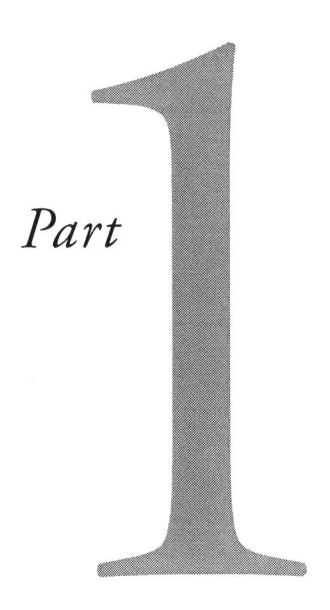

How does life begin?
        a tickle in the vesicle
        wanting to out

only in the case of rock, it is
the creak and groan of being
ram-rod hard
for six million years
night after night
rousing the stars
in their ancient outposts, wanting
the gnomon of his tribe—
there, a glyph on his sac
wanting him to dig for it
to dig it : to dig

except after eons of absolute desire
to erupt from the rules
of storm, wind, and ice,
        finally
to trickle up a fissure, creep
with bared teeth about to tear
into syllogism—

yet he is restraint, a
certain compliance,
since the passage must be negotiated
without haste, step by step
mount until properly seated
on horse, with patience
and forbearance
and a slight weakening of hope
spot a finale, then . . .

      (defense de cracher)

the first word
    curls his lips
      with its mime,
its meme:
life
the way it must begin
if it is ever ready to—

bear in mind
a numskull is a
mineral deposit
beetling eternity
in its empty sockets—
remember he is that,
with nothing
nothing
if for a mouth,
the first the thing vocal;

that metabolized
during the aion of rock, vigilant
to the horizon
for signs of the laws of
life coming. . .
yet they never did, nor life;

he was made for
a thousand deaths before
and this the eternity

    learned, it earned
    and vastly dispersed
    in one last place
        heart or soul.

      ◆ ◆ ◆

So the mind must trundle along
    with the workers on
        mid-year holiday to enjoy its,
        or else goes rancid
        with the butter of its own milk

they, paraded in their languid best,
    pockadot handkerchiefs and striped blazers
        pockets of palliatives for a dyspeptic stomach
        snake oil happiness
        a prospect of life unending
        with nothing to end for

    a pretense of charm marches
        an oblong shadow up the hill
            obsequious to any authority
            but its own
            and so the freedom
            of mind
            for a terrored glance at her truth

            that she, passing, stoops beneath
            a parasol, dazzling white
            breast, and asks,

            what did you mean
            starting up again

            when all you've ever said is nothing?

    Cra rrack

So he comes in hard fashion to note

      the importance of character and intellect,
how speech shares in respect
      of body armor, atmosphere, aura,
          all accoutrements of postponement

abound if more is needed
      to more acutely define
          the name of her political party's
          reform program
          for robbing the poor in the name of
          charity and fighting evil
          with beer-soaked sops

how she takes the strains of
      the national anthem as a flag flies:
          that is an acid test of her affection
          for if she is gullible
          she is not to be trusted

inasmuch as any fool can misname
what shepherds call sheep
known for wagging its tail
at its master

in a town
of infinite masters

❖ ❖ ❖

manufacture of rock:
      the compression of sediments washed from old mountains to the east, the moisture squeezed out, mud pressed to shale, fissured by catabasis.

❖ ❖ ❖

listen, the first word
can no longer be
a seismic murmur behind
a wall of glacier,
any word said
must now proclaim
the orgasm of body,

the man who
in that pre-dawn
came down
one foot planted
in the new field
held up just long enough
for the first projectile
to hit the earth
with a singularly loud expulsion—
there was a river
and there was a mountain
and there was a place
seeded with its own musky
history—of love!
    terra nova!
    nieuw pfalz!

❖ ❖ ❖

there, the town curls, nestled in
the old man's crotch
in need of a hind quarter,
one privileged
with the river that flows
a flexed vein
flooded by season—
flotsam of river
vagary of season
concordance of blood;

he, now heaped upon the hillside
kinks of big river elm gone slack
reclines on flanks
braced back like a chaise
and from their upright gets up
just before his retraction
into the pit of earth—
his eyes rove northwest
for the rounded tits of the Kaatskill—
and his single stone foot grows implanted
to put off necessity

Nieuw Pfalz
he calls his own name
again, *Nieuw Pfalz*—
cat's mews, feathers
nuance, innuendo
poorly remembered
holy and prophetic
words of the second coming:
love and death vie
on a bronze relief—names of
fire department mortalities,
police homicides, losses of
kin, memorial services,
abortions, deaths
by cause of excess, et cetera
et cetera;
death certificates, deaths
of ideals and ideologues,
the dead of the last wars
    (which one?)
the unclaimed dead or lost—
treasonous or faithful;

is not this an age redeeming
the joys of ephemera
    prolongation
    for that matter
    any but the end of it?

        otherwise if
        the word is slack
        slacker than fit,
        it must be transcribed,
        edited, proofed, composed,
        and (God willing) published,
        not in imitation of bronze—
        but the hard-core strap
        to hang yourself—
        the most quixotic
            ranks with hope
            of making the same world

                              over anew
                  but one that berms the spine
                  as silica does the stalk
                  sand and stone, striated
                  rockshod ice
                  from lava of smokerock

                  cirques and scarps

                              each is a rift
                                  on the unsubstantial
                              each is at risk
                                  for losing heart
                              each is a hope
                                  to avoid shame
                              each is a crime
                                  of evading denial
                              each is a sweet
                                  of the last addiction

        ❖ ❖ ❖

His gaze wanders and stretches
over her valley moraine,
clay of concupiscent
squaw cornfields
silted by river floods
the changing moon
and turned black antediluvian
soil as he imagines
inside the moist wall
contrived of rich humus
against him rubs with surprising
insistence he provide. . .

        ❖ ❖ ❖

Along the ridge pole of
the patent when the patent came,
an order delegated to the Twelve,
his desire to undress

Book One, *The Buial*

her in bedrooms,
woodsheds, other sheds, springhouses,
under shadbushes, in fields
redundant with purslane
wherever the sap would flow

        duzine
        twelve are the months of labor
        twelve are the houses of love
        twelve are the apostles of words
        twelve are the attributes of fools
        twelve are the days
        between birthing and dying

from Point Monogg
'in perpetuity' place was
gift in the first place, and
(though they traded off half
in short order rather than protracting)
the heel of his foot bore their seed
as he got their mortality
one after one under his stone

to the river point east
the lower belly swayed
where he liked to lick
nomenclature enough
to make her lie flat, a land
oozing with the title of it
a starved cat stuck in a tree
of a sacred grove
when all she wanted was
to growl low and long

        it must be rewritten thus
        in memory
        to be remembered
        made a real thing
        or else it is human law,
        or its fiction
        that decides for truth

❖ ❖ ❖

several springs and fallings/ pure springs of most excellent water
pleasantly distilling from their rockie foundations/ fresh water,
which streameth doune/ the Water is clear, fresh and fit for Brewing/
and such intersections and doublings of wood and Water/ with such
Fresh-waters running through the woods as I was almost rauished
At the first sight/ This river, running north along the valley to seek
the sea, comes to this hill

❖ ❖ ❖

   As he walks,
      he sees printeds
         many sorts,
            racing charts
            counterfeit prayers
            anodynes against mortality

   also: goods from the crag's still,
   (three actually, two for grape, one for apple)
   which Sam Gunt, federal revenuer,
   knew from the evidence of scree
   for secrets were never told
   in his presence but braggery, an odor or fragrance,
   an air women in town wore—

   he wrote,
   'a short walk west toward the caves,
   you find rock of great abundance
   in the shape of the Dionysian
   disguised to mislead the establishment
   of a clear map of the mind
   which is sought in retribution for brutality,'

   or he speculated,
   on redmen whose
   pilfering was herb to smoke,
   an inferior addict
   to some European capital's,
   and whose very ideal of vision
   was red eye of inflammation

> men soft as women
> the Lennie Lenapee

and that spirit, he took it,
must dribble each into
some infernal beaker
of self-choosing
under the stone ceiling,
whose judicious purge, the coil
throws to the ether
the hooch dubbed then
by the rock with its specific:
musk of
plump green belly.

The bush burns fay,
coolly, with a flame
that consumes nothing
as it goes,
a quavering force
in childhood,
where fear
is the wrong test
to fail

> (is it not that way
> with the hope
> that takes some
> irrefrangible sense from
> cocktail realism?)

❖ ❖ ❖

> Louis DuBois, dead & buried
> Christian Deyo, dead & buried
> Abraham Hasbrouck, dead & buried
> Andre LeFevre, dead &
> Pierre Deyo, dead buried
> Louis Bevier, dead
> Hugo Frere, ...
> each and every.

Nieuw Pfalz

yet lives their commence
industry, husbandry, valor
who understood their land
was bought, not given

'All creatures of a day
all dead long since,
some not remembered
even for a brief while
some turned into legends
some by now vanished
even from legends'

even their names in the throat—
a hooker ill-bred in
a library, a drawl
to make it look local
as a coffee cup's gargle
which the young couple, his sweaty paw
on her bare thigh as they laugh
and declaim—it is I
I who sailed with an angel
I who overheard their prayers and
suffered

❖ ❖ ❖

What glues flesh to mineral bone?

Love is similar
least of all to its ways

No purpose is more clear
than love is devious
without intending

to put a strait jacket
on congress,
an iron maiden
across the gate

Book One, *The Buial*

Yet love is sought
for its own sake
not because it betters
but for how it bends
truth without breaking
the willing lie inside

❖ ❖ ❖

From the first clot
the spade got,
the iron gored it
the hand flung it heavenward

as well the eye measured it—
then without greed—
righted the spine
to recall proverbs
about the rent
kept to its ways
day after day, morning, night—
through agora-culture
not penury of peltry

> *all things else
> the riddle of the heart—*

a voice devoid of
fact, force, and figure
begins to account for
the first installation
of a reverse tide
to what pinions a man
to the bedrock of his life
while he squirms to see
the jaws that
clamp his windpipe,

—that voice that gags
on mountain dust

n bended knee (on
a leather buskin)

❖ ❖ ❖

the two should stroll
down from the pamphleteers
advising a worker revolt,
clamber on soft moss
love has no single reason:
it is not the dew
that dries by noon,

as it spans
the two on sticky strands
to foretell
        no escape

❖ ❖ ❖

Vines run naturally
 ground doth naturally bring forth vines
the wild vines cover all the hills along the river like veins
I have seen whole pieces of land where vine stood by vine
and divers grape vines which though growing without culture in the very trough
of weeds and bushes were yet filled with bunches of grapes to tumescent
admirement
vines in many parts on the sea shore, bearing multitude of grapes, where one
would wonder they should get nourishment
    such abundance as where soever a man treads, they are ready to
    embrace his foot
    vine in bigness of a man's thigh

❖ ❖ ❖

Afterward, she remembers
to call it independence
when she needs a gun to get
the ratty school bus engine
number 28, up over black ice
bucking uphill on loose clutch
(call maintenance on that)

she utters her last syllable
of woe
to night's dead body,
the heartbeat winter weak,
and begone,
once and for all begone!
Do not come again
you are not welcome

That is her sole purpose
in destroying night
with the mortar shell
of a bad timing chain,
for all that, she slams into
no other but him—
looking reflective
in the windscreen
of her silver locket

       she asks that he obey,
her stiletto of ice
under Berenice's comb,
               obey
a wind blown over
the hell's mouth
a diesel motor
shredding the highway's bed
      as though to roll in it

       Cold fingers grip her calves
from shifting the lousy gears
damning the Ryan girl
for not fixing them,
turn to damn creation
for including her,

          then desists
          to light
a cigarette
to keep from going star-crazy
like he would like her to. . .

    that warmth that in life persists in death is
    as warm in life,
    just as cold in death is no colder than life,
    that warmth that passes over
    the mineral brow
    of his highness the marauder
    she comes to love,
    under veil sought
    for intrinsic squalor

    the warmth of new life:
    solar warmth or saline warmth,
    oxygen warmth by night,
    salt from the warm inland sea
    blanched before the ice age,
    weighs and disposes . . .
    in exegesis of
    the saline creature
    whose deposit lines
    the bones
    examining him.

❖ ❖ ❖

Let him walk among women
   rasping in long, low satin gowns
   while arbutus and anemone
   laurel and bloodroot
   rhododendron
   slender nut grass
   brush his bony ankles
   causing prickles to spring up
   late April heat;

Let him walk among women
   while elder, strawberry, and clover
   June beetles and black locust
   catalpa and Rigosa rose
   dandelion peony
   tulip tree swamp iris

\Book One, *The Buial*

moisten her emanations of flesh
in a great sigh, heaved
and so wrought the world
into frenzied existence

❖ ❖ ❖

So much for deceit. So much for lying. You hide a key for yourself, under some special flap. That way, you can always escape. Don't think I'm ignorant of how you lie to me constantly. I've never aspired to being a slave. I'd rather be one of those who line the street, in appreciation of your bravery and skill. It is my ambition to be determined by a man. In your regard, I continue to respect your prowess, though much is done with mirrors. Nonetheless, I admit being intrigued and am prepared to coalesce, however bizarre that sounds. I am, your Oemome.

❖ ❖ ❖

When the Ferris Company, hired to manage the show, inspected the steel chains on Pete Novalis, they found nothing amiss. No loose links, all bolts locked tight. The chains were reputed to be strong enough to hold a bull elephant and had been used in the Barnum Circus for that purpose until auctioned off. Pete seemed the picture of equanimity as he let them lower him into the eight-foot pit that the Star Hose Company dug especially for the occasion. There, as he stood chained on the bedrock, looking up through his custom goggles, men began to throw shovelsful of dead sand over him. Slowly it mounted and in a few minutes was up to his breast, then covered his neck to his chin. In another moment, only the shock of his black hair was visible. Then he was gone. The men continued to hurl sand at a faster pace until the hole was a mere indentation marking Pete N's temporary gravesite. Lanterns swung from stone altars constructed out of the white New York conglomerate of the mountain. A warm breeze brought a balm to the night air. The girls of the Normal School had been let out to frolic one last time before the first killing frost. Their tittering was all there was to be heard as everyone held their breath, even the principal. After what seemed an eternity, during which a screech owl entertained the audience with its piercing moan, there were sounds of grappling from under the sand. Vague syllables emerged from the sand, oracular and menacing. Immediately the crowd was divided as to a course of action. Some wanted to extract Pete before he breathed his last, while others felt it was part of the act. Tensions grew and the would-be diggers had already assumed their positions when one of Pete's hands appeared under the surface, then the other. In a minute, the crown of his head came through under a caul of sand. When his chin got up, he spat a large amount from his mouth and let his goggles be tended to. Before he could stop them, the Ferris men were finishing the disinterment and dusting him off like a resurrected soul. He was then helped by two attendants out to Budd's Hotel, where they put summer tourists up for three dollars a night. Before he disappeared, he turned and waved weakly to the cheering crowd of townspeople and school children. The price of their admission was more than rewarded by their amazement at what the human spirit can accomplish when it is strong and free.

❖ ❖ ❖

S. Judkins, U.S.M. Stageline, Daily Line—Sunday Excepted. Leaves N.P. Daily at 8:30 A.M. Passing through Ohioville, Lloyd, Highland (all colonies), returning leaves post office Po'keepsie, 1:30 p.m. Orders left at the News Office, second door north of Smith's Dining and Saloon. Passengers from trains and steamboats can meet the stage at the Ferry House at precisely 2 p.m. to cross the river.
—Samuel Judkins, Proprietor

List of Fares

New Paltz to Poughkeepsie ....60 cents
    "   " to Highland ....50 cents
    "   " to Lloyd .... 30 cents
    "   " to Ohioville .... 15 cents

❖ ❖ ❖

    As he walked he read on the stage schedule
    how foreign blood bled with home-bred,
    walked white with red, red with white,
    separate, they commute
    in nature as she had it, all red
    now he showed his Indian trick and
    came to think of the next escape, what time
    or where, until he lost the purpose
    or forgot, speaking of it
    whether red or white, white or red

        red is how you speak
        red is how you live
        red is how you are

    Being foreign himself
    he spoke this or that way, which way
    though no one took his word for it
    though on the third try
    the stigma was noted, excited
    to pursue and kill

        red is what he thought
        red is what he said
        red is what he was

❖ ❖ ❖

New Paltz Independent, February 3, 1883.

Three female students of the Normal School were treated for frostbite by Dr. Williams at his offices in Water Street. They had been on the lawn of the school, witnesses to the marvelous travelling act of Peter Novalis. Unfortunately preparations had taken over six hours. One of them, Sarah Bevier, became hysterical with

Book One, *The Buial*

pain and accidentally set fire to the building when she overturned Dr. Williams' gas autoclave. Because the entire fire brigade was to be found at Budd's Hotel, celebrating the event with Mr. Novalis, the office burned to the ground, including the contract the town board had signed for Mr. N's services.

◆ ◆ ◆

Normal School confidential report: P. N. is obsessed with disorder. Mishaps are drawn to him as files to a magnet. His feelings seem quixotic in character. He tilts after windmills and consequently, never knows what comes next. After the fire destroyed his contract, he took it as a personal loss that absolved him of not having to explain himself to anyone. He was allowed to walk away from it and fleeced the town in return. From town to town, he is able to find new acts when his old ones go dead, impaled by some terrible angel stalking him like Caleb. There are reasons to believe he craves revenge for the town's attitude toward him. There is a peculiar magnetism, as we know, between desire and event.

◆ ◆ ◆

      The beginning isn't obvious
      either as first cause,
            or impulse to speak,
      because it lives on and must
      found an expression or
      until it happens, must
      be the question
      of how the cherry bowl
      will be picked

      and whether to find
      in every peculiarity its specific
      depth recovered
      by dint of that will
      against memory's erasure
      to mute voice

            there, the story is already
            a fall
            from the beginning
            as it has a precursor
            existing as
            no story
            ever yet told

      wet with force
      one eye seeing the other
      lying, stars emerge
      like a scent of hers

coming up with the dew
naked perspiration,
a laborious approach
from momentary amnesia
of an entire world;

this is the wait
in the doctor's office, only here, put off
until beauty comes in
         (as she does a little after)
strong and fat, aglow
with sunset from the stone window

◆ ◆ ◆

Come, the pit said,
trust me:
suck air

from the throat chakra
and speak sibilantly

of predicates of
common purpose—

do you hear what syllables
together can conjure
subdivisions
which transcend
the common

as one divides
two
and is half
of two already?

        which is what the pit says
        which is why he digs

                dark
                and a distinctly warped
                Jurassic rock
                fault

◆ ◆ ◆

The Star Hose Company has two wagons but only one in use. The other brigade, the Ulster Ladder Company, is too poorly equipped for even a fire that would extinguish on its own accord. The better of the two stands high on its six-foot wheels, with iron-clad rims. Whenever it sets out, there is a painful rumble underfoot that worries citizens. In summer, a persistent cloud of gray dust hangs just over it and pursues the engine like a demon. Dust has become a great nuisance on the porches of the district. It is tracked inside everywhere. In winter, only the snow obstructs it from spreading further. This said, our town can be proud of our up-to-date machinery to safeguard life or property. One useless wagon doesn't add a single stain to our town's repute.

◆ ◆ ◆

        The Quakers came after Albert Steen
        invited the apple orchard
        on the north side
        where those to the path,
        passed the grist mill

and must have known others who
didn't come to a rock vault
a hundred paces
east of the trail head
beside a shale pit
where a scrim of knotweed,
kept trysts secret, in the sun
of aboriginal love

Pete takes a woman there
a woman of knowledge
who knows to murder,
and there dies a dozen deaths
and a dozen resurrections
before the fatal thirteen

◆ ◆ ◆

        In broad view the graveyard
        down wind from the Dutch houses
        squats on an ancient precinct

Nieuw Pfalz

loved by Manitou, the One,
would raise a serpentine flame
there, on the same mid-winter eve
each year for a tribal palaver,
half-grown braves dance
along with elders stripped,
bodies blood ochre and coraldine,
up to their groins
she held them melting in heat
(30 degree of frost or more)
there cast until depleted,
piscine, they swam in her primal sea

—there, several girls of an upper grade
who chose the February eve for dance
had faint spells and chill bumps
flare up the young white thighs
where they quavered with feline desire

❖ ❖ ❖

I saw right through you when you asked about the Dutch names. Then I knew where you stood on colonialism. Such a saturnine temper. Kill is their word for river. Where does such antagonism go? They may be slow and persistent but do not trust them. They build stone houses along waterways. A Dutchman will never forget. Take Director Kieft, for example. How in 1642, he relished the entrails of his enemy removed one by one, and watched them burned before him on the stake. It was he who made the Pfalz run red during the slaughter of the Esopus. As French, they are clever and industrious as farmers and make the earth fruitful. You could respect what they accomplish with shovel and hoe. If the cost of commerce was murder, they are bereft of human kindness as ever walked the earth.

❖ ❖ ❖

The force that
binds a man is welded
invisibly
to his calcine home
an embryo soul—
if one and the same
sedimentary

gives voice
to the soundness

Book One, *The Buial*

of its glosses

on his secret hum
a flattened thumb—
rock your heels
grind it up

◆ ◆ ◆

During the past week considerable excitement has prevailed in our village on account of the presence of Internal Revenue Officers and the discoveries of concealed whisky. Deputy collector H.R. Wilcox and another officer came at noon digging for the hidden treasures. Charles Freer was employed to handle the pick and shovel. In the distillery, an empty apple barrel was found a foot underground, and large whisky barrels. Next the house situated just in the rear of the distillery was visited and a trench found where five barrels had evidently been placed and a smell of liquor remained. But no barrels were found. On Thursday, five cords of wood were removed from the distillery and another trench was found which had evidently contained five more barrels of the precious liquid. But none was there now. No less than six revenue officers were present on Thursday. When digging was resumed, half a barrel of liquor was found about nine inches underground in a corner. This liquor tested at four above proof.

◆ ◆ ◆

        The glottal stop
        at the hump
            in saving Watch Hill's backside's
            a big blood bath,
            not bad if you

            haste, people
            watch for the train:
            weeklies from Manhattan
            mail, potato
            from Long Island,
            hens from the Bronx
            orders of Scilician sundries
            raisons salt cod pipe tobacco
            schnapps candies ladies' scent
            veterinary medicinals

     Summers sprints
          from
          Phillies Bridge
          to the train before you

Nieuw Pfalz

        later
        winter blinds you
        with much more soul,
        Tutilltown, maybe
        is to what you hear
        that loose iron piece
        idiocy or old age

❖ ❖ ❖

In the stillness
behind the flashpan of the still,
the parties congregate—
to worship separate vintages
Democrats in back
Republicans
       in front
       of the register,
       all drinking

each lost in illusion—
power summits
life endowed with remembrance
in bronze—

yet for each the word
speaks
from the bone hollows
forbidding any deceit
of imagination

and has men out
       their truth
in front of the terror
of lies

              yet lets the rock
              peak to
              the man
              in a distinct
              vocable

       the man's
       own
       as he was
       as clear as rock

       when each, man
       and rock fecundate
       each,
       as it be

❖ ❖ ❖

'We don't think the same. I used to believe we were just different and more so then. If you ask, I couldn't say when. As you know, I was content to listen to the songbirds in the trees. One day you woke with a scheme and were off. It isn't for the money you took without asking. God knows, there is real money I could have made. I've never had the heart to beg. Perhaps we differ there too, in our estimation of love. You are dear to me when you know feeling is the essence of life.'

❖ ❖ ❖

       The second time the escapologist came to town
       was at the Devil's swim hole,
       above Poor Farm, remnants of the orchard
       Steen build many years before the aqueduct
       severed the cinder road to Duck Pond and
       shrouded the creek in bleak mortared rock

       It captivated minds since fame was his
       from the Albany circus—
       incarcerated in an oak chest doubled in chain,
       nailed shut by the sheriff's deputies before
       they set the thing up with a torch

             men who wanted him
             to lose and hated him for not

       The tighter the noose
       the more his imagination was there
       to mold the key of it
       for a good impression
       for the forge

On a blustery day in April,
before the first monkshood,
the sheriff, Bill Jaspers, known more
for good times than killing
lowered the flaming casket
[Marcellus Casket Company
Syracuse, New York,
Manufacturers]
the trademark branded in the shape
        of a skull
sank in the swollen surge of
the effluent alpine pool
deeper than a depth chamber

the Lenape weighted themselves
with boulders of quartzite
        —into the abyss
           until vast heavens beyond
           stars gleamed without obstruction
sank 20 feet into invisibility
for which the naked eye had paid
two cents
to miss the essential feat

mind rapt
in the sibylline trance
that once sired a river sylph
from the ridge, his instep,

        for they knew
        the word is
        no second thought
        but a flash
        of sentience

        coming back
        from less stupefied
        surrounds

observe: the silken thread
enlacing the coffin in a shimmer

all or none panicked
at the burial grounds,
     to witness
to the latest in the name of art

Overhead, the midges assumed
truculent pattern, some took as a sign
Pete's mortal soul had business ahead,
from others, a cyclone of valediction

and just as it bemoaning the fate
lifted toward the empyrean,
a young girl's voice cried out—

Pete's head in the open casket
was haloed in deciduous light
though bound by chains to the wood chest,
burst by a small explosive
dissembled from the waist down
thighs and knees reddened by the act

orange canvass swim trunks raggy,
goggles around his head,
   P. himself,
barely strained for breath

    thrust, an image
    of imagination in
    a town imagined
    in words of
    an imagined poet

    who lives
    and dies with
    imagination—
    place imagined
    words imagined

    the voice only
    nearing
    that inflection

and basking in a glory
a blush on schoolgirls' faces,
chains galore but death no longer
freed from the past, his past,
the past of Nieuw Pfalz, imagined
in a great act of an escape artist
who wants changes
with each character, and v.v.—

in that disguise, he walks metaphor dripping
across the astonished town
board, for the purse promised
should be contested
as the contract on his person is
bound for the early stage for Po'keepsie
where he might divine the next act.

❖ ❖ ❖

Dead sand came from the Curtis Brick Company factory on the east bank. They hauled it over five counties with a team of six. In those days there was stiff competition among brickmakers, and Curtis amplified his fortune with a mix of brick crumbs, as they called them, and river silt. The char of the brick poisons all life. Children don't play in it. It was the mix of the Deyo Brothers when in 1872 they laid the downtown sidewalks. Merrill's Dry Goods had a precipitous drop in summer sales, before they were removed to widen the street. By then, several businesses, including the cobbler, Mister Clifford, had closed.

❖ ❖ ❖

Sorry to be a bother. It's the rent. Do you expect a girl with two jobs to have time for her journal? I don't want to point a finger, but if fame isn't what you're after—you've said so—it's an immortality far more dangerous. I don't have the luxury of thinking about posterity. It's the past that fills me with longing. I hear myself weep in the middle of the night as if from someone else's pain.

❖ ❖ ❖

The emblem of

three stools at the bar
three women
at Budd's,
one a Titaness

Book One, *The Buial*

a fourth jar
for some divine salve

that preserves
eternal
measure

to keep the town
in place—

above, three others'
loyal judgment

falls
like a cloak

to arrest
the shoulder

as it leans over
the abyss

                         it must remain
                         unsaid that
                         each syllable
                         is a rebel

                         against aggregate
                         order in song,

                         it must be feared
                         for revolutionary
                         strains

                         never trusted
                         to be real
                         since its bounds
                         on the fly
                         go beyond story

Part 2

A deeply thumbed elemental,
sleeping alone
while life goes on in the other room,
an incessancy without peace

to begin the game of
life: rock
water, fire, a child's
querulous murmur
against which ears must be stopped—
      fist, palm, forefinger
      rock splinters match
      paper publicizes rock
rock resumes its identity as rock

Burn the paper, destroy
the disinformation,
let the finger wind erectile
adornment for an evening sky
feeling toward the rock's plinth
ahead of patient abstinence

Let the rock speak.
      Let the fire yearn.
Let fresh paint on the sign

Book One, *The Buial*

     read and be wider read,
     than reclusive calcium
     who ossifies west each day
     in a journal of solitude
           he writes from anonymous cause

◆ ◆ ◆

To begin, a dream of Novalis.
  The empty drum rolls first to one edge of the raft, then to the other, finding a balance-point now here, now there, dependent on the water's whim, fickle and without regard to music, now it postures manly on the edge of the partially sunken stage, as if to dictate the laws of inertia, now, with the advent of grace, it is freed from certain annihilation, now as its raft lurches against an adjoining ice floe, it falls motionless on the precise center, and then as the jam suddenly gives way, it is catapulted into that dark oblivion of which no witness speaks.

◆ ◆ ◆

Minutes on the Novalis cause: a meeting in the Academy rectory:

  Professors' opinions were divers. Professor Coffman, of the physics department, averred that a secret means exists to corrupt the chain's metallic strength, to the point of liquefaction. To rip them apart then is not difficult. Professor Hamilton, of the biology department, supposes Abe uses a life-suspension technique, acquired in his childhood with the Lenape Indians. With the method, he could survive up to 30 minutes. Professor Jones, of the history department, lectured on priestly arts of the Lenni, the 'woman's tribe,' that inhabited the region. Though skeptical, the school's faculty felt a divine call in Peter Novalis when it came to escapology. Professor Lane, of the geology department, noted men have sought the depths interior to rock since prehistoric times, and the deeper to fathom, the more attractive it is.
      Caitlin Henderson, recording secretary

◆ ◆ ◆

Your plots are lame. They don't mean a thing. They have been thoroughly contrived and are filled with contradictions. You may thrive in that condition, but I'm afraid I can't. It makes me ill. It's always on my mind, scheming up ways that are no better. It's an obsession, my doctor says. Your hidden talent to alter identity makes it impossible for me to find mine. One mask after the next—I get tired of pulling them down. I don't believe we could live together.

◆ ◆ ◆

Some thought Peter
    the devil
    or some subaltern thereof
at Whorters
the other All Souls'
they told he could win out against
    whatever contraption
    they could put him in

    because of a pact
    granting disputed powers
    far outside the normal
    mortal ones

    at the price of
    his immortal soul

so when he showed up
for the Sunday after Easter
at the Reformed Church
no one sat near
his pew
save one small girl
in a checked bonnet
who kept looking
under his cloak
for hooves

◆ ◆ ◆

John Burroughs, who thought the town forgot its destiny, walked over the mountain to visit the old Steen orchard. Albert Steen's scheme had been enlarged, then abandoned. On a brilliant October day, Burroughs stood admiring the last frostbitten apples hanging desirously from the top branches. While in the process of pulling out a small, ivory-handled revolver he kept handy for such purposes, he noticed a native species of junco (junco aikeni) he had not seen. Crediting his readiness to good fortune, he took aim as the bird flew directly overhead. His shot was true and he stooped to admire the still-warm specimen. Then, straightening again, he dropped the body into a squat leather side-pouch and walked home, before lunching on cheese and clear spring water from the mill pond.

◆ ◆ ◆

The Independent, February 29, 1884
For the first time in not very many years, NP has been visited by a destructive fire. The old Academy building, which attracted pleasant associations, has fallen to the flames. At midnight on Friday, with the mercury down nearly to zero degrees of frost, the cry of fire went out with the ringing of the Academy bell. Soon, the church bells aroused a great commotion in the village and men from all parts rushed to the scene of conflagration. The progress of the flames was rapid. A stiff wind blew in from the northwest and sparks were soon flying over a great portion of the neighborhood. —Nothing but the snow on the roofs prevented other buildings from catching fire. A small party of fifteen or so guests had been invited by Mr. Partington to spend the evening. They had sat down to tea about 10:30 o'clock. There were Mr. And Mrs. J.J. Hasbrouck, Mr. And Mrs. Oscar C. Hasbrouck, Miss LeFebre, Edward Smiley, Jacob Deyo, Gertrude Elting, Miss Minnie Scott of Newburgh, and Miss Gillespie of Montgomery.

❖ ❖ ❖

Not to seek sin with an arc wider
than the swath of Carthage
but subject to centripicity
suppose in its own conflagration
an impudent question
begging the answer

to confess ambition to Meister
Auchmoody, fresh from Alsace,
a craving for carnal knowledge
of case and article
unrepentant
of transgression to an extent
practiced beyond human vice,
—for from the scourge of his own mouth
dragon's teeth fell to the earth—
entangled by warm hands—
and so the word broadcast
like an ill-humor
only in this case more corrupt

fire
the fire!
the fire leaps over its blue head
to a third story frame,
roils the wood canopy
and spreads tidings
of its conversion
unto the cupola—

skewers the oaken flange
on a spree of rapturous consent
that embraces the narcissus of
reckless design
in a spasm
of transcendence
before scruples
in the fabric of
limit or
        finality
stoned in the glory of . . .
an inhalation lavishly
condemned to its maw
        pure oxygenation
        fount
                of eternal youth

But what pops to
the posture is
a dog braced to attack
and all at once pounces—
        at a dozen victims at once
        a demon hound who
        divides in seven
        at will

When the jaws close for lost
adrenaline, the lips
crease where the flames licked,
and the floor of the place afire
even the rock is fire, and fire
        the rock,

while gauzy lace of the hemlocks
partly deluded by the eastern blight,
bursts spontaneously into sympathy—
which is love apparent—
the impassively white powder
is spurted in orange spumes and
from gassy resins
of conquest, match over paper,

Book One, *The Buial*

match over rock can hold
a middle finger to heaven,
and the game revolves
around a languid amble
to the playground,
along the pathway of eternal flux
every thing already there—
swings, slide, sandbox, and
        seesaw
no longer able to keep
a burning dislike of dissimulation
apart—gone, lost to love in which
opposition is weakness and
weakness, a shudder in conquest

    —the errant soul of mountain that day
had need for no bright-eyed sentinel,
the daily news came to the townspeople
in the event of the poem

        Degrees of fire

        dragon-fire
        forge-fire
        hearth-fire
        candle-fire
        devil-fire
        infernal fire

Spent before the carnal act
has reared to completion,
an elemental appetite
prematurely appeases
a voracious imagination,
suddenly the tragedy
in dearth of motive or intent,
presumes the form
of a gas bubble, monstrously
luminous, its bay hollow
from the middle out, light
without a source—holy light!
    and instantly subsides
    in a parody of apostasy

        over the prostituted body
        of the school that kneels
        crumpled on the earth
        unaware her business
        has concluded . . .

❖ ❖ ❖

I do know why I can't stand you writing me. You tell about your lovers to have me feel heartache and guilt. I don't believe in voyeurism. It's like a narcosis because you want more. I would rather commit sin than subscribe to v. Nonetheless, I haven't forgotten stories need to be told. At least it was that way before kiss and tell, when people kept secrets. The temptations are different, but should I enjoy the obvious? Does it open doors?
      –your former student

❖ ❖ ❖

Time and again, they are women who look to confess. As he appoints himself confessor. Then when they start on private matters, he turns apart. They are abandoned and their strength often fails them for lack of same. This is his method, as Doctor Augustine pointed out. He can't see his failures, but what is it? I tell you by way of warning, because I don't want you going to the druggist.

❖ ❖ ❖

        During Quaker meeting, Fay
        would take glutinous breaths
        while he declaimed
        with pontifications
        on the exchange value of land
        in the valley, the cancerous threat
        of competition from the east bank's
        extra crop of corn

        glory it was, to the glory
        he added, of a man
        to mend what he hath sawn,
        prudent mercantile loans in
        the good Locke's marriage
        of government and
        corpse-oration
        that would culture a second Eden

>   when what it will effect
>   turns the apple to jack

> *the risk of the word*
>   *is untruth*
> *the risk of untruth*
>   *is shame*
> *the risk of shame*
>   *is weakness*
> *the risk of weakness*
>   *is aggression*
> *the risk of aggression*
>   *is despair*

General Vaughn, the miscreant who proved it to King George, set the torch. Governor Clinton, mired in Newburgh, passed through the Pfalz, stopping for supper at the house of Abrum Hasbrouck, where he enjoyed a maize meal dinner made by Elizabeth Deyo for the occasion. Jonathan, Abrum's brother, followed a company to the rear. If the Pfalz river hadn't been fouled by autumn rains, Clinton could have rescued Kingston. As it was, everyone, young and old, made off with what they had and left before Vaughn's henchmen finished lighting. The fire could be seen from Shawangung where the rebel encampment stood. The foe ran off quickly and light, for V. was coward and feared a counter-attack.

The Independent, October 17, 1884
In the two dozen books rescued from the charred library of the Academy School was one curious signature of eight pages that, according to librarian Rosalind Haviland, was written in 1732 in the solitude of the fortress of Sonnenstein.   The preface tells that a certain Douzetemps descended from the most militant French Huguenots, the Desert Dwellers. He was unjustly incarcerated in Germany for a decade for an unspecified offence. The very name of the prison has been questioned: Sonnenstein [Sun Stone] suggests hermetic symbolism. Mrs. Haviland was unable to locate it in what remained of the card catalogue. The prose was succinct, in the manner of early Dutch merchants who brought Christian ways to New Holland.

    Journal of Ajib the red

    Left Manitou
    whose god smells human
            gone north
    a small forsaken Golgotha
    breath full and down
               ward
    where redmen drink white water
    firewater brandy

Nieuw Pfalz

white brandy water
                      shake dour
visions of dark slaves
Ignorant
circumsized mohammed
                      stands
on the temple of the grapeless god
where
even the wild beast flees
before the fire
                      of this one
the Lord only loves
a quiet body

                      To the east
the devil walks on the map
when snow falls
the town comes alive
Here no man finds
much the same for long,
they honor him
exile & a place
the sun leaves,
this rock alone
in darkness waits,
                      penitent
Wild geese above north
hiss
skidding down again
with remarkable speed

Ammad Ajib comes one day
each year the same
his lean-to east
along the devil's walk
3000 feet above God's waters
drained from a lake of tears
the Hudson
some 300 years
since the half-moon
Henry's secretary
said drug
          'more than all is a disturbing
          element was the appetite of the
          redmen for intoxicating drink'

Book One, *The Buial*

& beyond, under cloud
sweet Sugerloaf, his lookout
on dawn flaring
when time could be brought
by his tribe again . . .

Not always do they worship
eunuchs
around the gate
of trunks of trees, Enkida,
slick with glowing insects

I threw myself to the rock
in terror,
one-armed, for the weak
to lean on,
green eyes

In preparing flames
smoke is her veil
virgin of both sexes
under his eyes
on green moss
they were fed jerkin,
sunflower seed, squash,
cattle & goat,
wheat, family records
opening tombs of the fathers
& always, always crying
the same chant
svale, svale
as white fire is
the passion of
what organ
of speech?

'durst not trust them. . .
        making shows of love'
the river sees a thin ribbon of
light a campfire southeast
today caught an updraft
to the notch
6 miles from his kitchen
where he prepares celebrants
in mad laughter, now
touching his flesh
an accidental return
to the Great Year,

        and one old man who saw
        'women clothed in hemp, red copper tobacco pipes &
        other things of copper they did wear about their necks'
        had his bridge mutinying
        the crew thirsting revenge
        on perpetrating untruth

        lies do make time
        look sweet
        in his decadent book
        clouds may oil the rock
        but it is still chill

◆ ◆ ◆

There are days I need musks and mints. In order to feel whole again. You must look at me as if I were morally astray. The loss of a little propriety is what you don't like. You get so high and mighty when there's as much as a syllable out of place. For Jesus' sake, there are days I wrestle to get the door open and out on the street. I don't want to think what's in ambush. That's what I learned about Indian justice: speak your mind and mind your own.

◆ ◆ ◆

    What was the water after
                         but knowledge
    as it crept on fingers over
    the river's shoulder
    up one course of narrow stone stairs
        as Normal School
        shuddered at the touch
        so liquid with engine
        and pregnant with
        consequences of commerce
        this time of night

    but he eggs her on to class
    say, on oceanography
    or fluid dynamics
    that she irresistibly loves

    . . . or if not knowledge of the mind,
    what is high is too high,

       then of the flesh,
       for flesh was one thing he loved
       to lap up, a reptilian tongue
       a viper who could feed
       moist saline thoughts
       in concert with the means

       —both want to ravage
       the brackish marsh
       to see which monsters lurked
       in the acrobatic prescriptions

       . . .and if not of mind or of flesh
       the heart was what the river sought
       since it had none
                           and craved
       its romantic staves

Then, as the river's desirous lips
       reach the girls' gymnasium
       it instantly froze at the sight,
       and ice of a full inch formed
       and a curious optical effect
       made the moon duller,
       as in a glass—
                          farmers rode
       miles overland to view
       the singular event
       which fortunate town children saw
       just before bedtime stories

The Quakers found its light
                         ominous
       and wanted to abjure
                         its clairvoyance
                         of purpose
                         not unsusceptible
                         to distraction
                         by any human means

        but in the moon's waning
        a mild thaw
        brought prophecy of
        the second coming to an end

Later that same year, spring's late floods
        bolted into cold tempestuous summer
        so corn from the Indian fields
        was smutty

        the ground had been lustful
        for the stalk and the silk, lactal,
        sucked   until they lost turgor
        to flocks of sheep
        geese and doves
        the pageant of multiplication
        that trumped the succulence
        of a mud-caked banquet

That year the stills brewed
        'ghost-eater' of the caves
        marketed at six percent above proof

❖ ❖ ❖

Mary Easton drowned in the flood last Friday. Kenneth Lefevre found her body in his lower field near Phillies ferry Easter morning. A thin snow dressed the corpse and, as Mr. Lefevre later reported, he assumed it was an angel. She had been carried a mile and a half downstream by the tremendous torrent of water. Her wool overcoat was weighted with ancient river rocks from the State Museum in Albany. After examination, Doctor Williams ruled it a suicide. Investigators at the Normal School, where she was a student, read in Mary's journal that she lived in dread of a vision she had on a class trip to the mountain caves. There was also her written apology for the theft. Later that month, Reverend Dunton Albritton, from Hoagburg, was found dead in his barn a week after preaching at the School. Foul play was suspected, but all eventually agreed it was accidental. He had tripped from a loft onto sheep fencing, where he dangled headfirst for an hour until suffocated.

❖ ❖ ❖

Book One, *The Buial*

The steel frame bridge went up in 1914 but before, the fording was near Water Street. In 1845, the town hired a ferry for the daylight hours and for emergencies. The ferryman's hut stood near the pier on the west bank, below the LeFevre corn field. In 1888, a mad year, the ferry capsized in a winter flood, drowning three passengers and a dog. The toll was then a ha'penny per passenger, a penny for a horse. Isaac Hasbrouck, son of Jacob, was the ferryman and it was he who retrieved dog's body in the muck of Jeremiah DuBois' lower squash field. Once, a baby girl was born on it, of one Jessica Deyo. A midwife happened to be crossing at the time. Thunder and lightning burst overhead with the infant's first cry. Townspeople took it as a sign of a future in crime. Caleb, the child's name, went mad believing he was a large landowner.   People would see him in the mountain walking their fields in a red hunting jacket. No one knew where he slept but most tolerated (to a degree) his innocent trespass. He disappeared after All Souls and the next spring was found in a block of ice during the harvest at Lake Mohonk.

◆ ◆ ◆

Dear Albert,
You were a thing I had to give up if I wanted to breathe again. You were so large, after the war and the success with your apple trees, that there wasn't any air for my lungs. I owed it to myself. The heartache is obvious but the accomplishment of duty brings great respite. Can you acknowledge that? You didn't really think I'd fall in love, did you, or was it a hope? I'll be with another man, but a ring doesn't change the heart. I have been rash with many, but I feel fresh resolve. Will you return what of mine you have?
   —your Bea.

◆ ◆ ◆

Is love than death stronger?

One burr can make a difference
if it's under a saddle

One surmise can kill a county
if they're believers

The surmise is lime, kiln-baked
by Dr. Pound's method, pulverized
under a two-ton grindstone
that yields a superior product
market-valued at 36 cents the long ton

Lime is crucial to the

Nieuw Pfalz

carbonation of cement,
rock with rock mixed
without which to sell
people would be without cities

So the surmise grows rich
filled by a deep conviction
in its inherent value
that entitles it and it alone
to distribution
        of wealth
        according to Smith

As the surmise fills itself
with crimes of greatness
the nation becomes ideal,
a dream dreamed
        by dreamers
forgetting the wild horse
on whose back it sits—
idle of its peril

◆ ◆ ◆

It is a resting place, I suppose. I have no other facts. That's the effect of good country air. The risk is so clear that it refutes the premises. But that is why one gives himself up. I saw what you wrote the last days. It's God-awful. Where does the stuff come from? I'm not consoled by your philosophies. The pain is real, searching for an identity woefully weak in print. The hunger in people rises with their riches, like the Goulds, the Livingstons, the Fultons. Their clans pervade the plateaus.

◆ ◆ ◆

You keep asking where I'm writing from. Don't follow. I'm alone and you can't find me. Life is strange. I tripped over a gravestone of Mildred Elting, and immediately I formed a picture of myself in your dining room, down to the least particular. The image was of her on her porch, taking in the salutary air, the dappled sunlight warming her skin, thinking of the fire that killed her grandson. I might stay on the mountain with a mineral lake—a sink hole whose unplumbed depth frightens me. I don't see people anymore, they so tax the nerves. Women get summer jobs picking blueberries, they are abundant on the rock ledges.

◆ ◆ ◆

Book One, *The Buial*

Indian pepper thick in muck
stands guard over the silver stack
and stalks the brook with a silent eye
to what is amiable in custody
but who gaze beneath a deacon's hood
observe Priapus' noontime food

◆ ◆ ◆

Lecture by P. Auchmoody, given at the Academy, April 16, 1882

It is an excellent thing when men's religions makes them free-hearted and open-handed, scorning to do a thing that is paltry and sneaking. Introspection may be carried to excess and become morbid; but there is a world within as well as without, and the one is as important as the other. A thought that is not heart-bred never cannot result in spiritual things. Glitter without warmth a most helpless thing. The reason why people grumble at long sermons is because they do not feed on them. Very seldom the hungry man murmurs at having too big a meal.

◆ ◆ ◆

Why people pay
to witness
the superhuman
with their own eyes

an incomprehension
thrust upon
a disbelieving
childish mind

in awe
of the trials
imagination
dreams up

to become the man
by whose labors
a real event
flows forth

Nieuw Pfalz

❖ ❖ ❖

What do you say you did with the poem you wrote me? I don't know how you felt when you sent it. Please tell the reason I was the object, now you have established you were only the medium. There's enough superstition around to make me sick, and I don't see why you have to add to the sum. Is there a more obvious explanation?

❖ ❖ ❖

      As a commentary on Albert Smiley's
      geophysical work
      concerning the hidden methane fissure
      under the Trapps near Warwarsing Pike
      at which various jackadaws would try
      their hand at second-rate prophecy.
      P. Novalis decided to give a vintage
            performance
            in the genre
            of which he was proclaimed master:
      escapology

      on a day significantly July
      a slight northerly
      lifted up the gaze
      toward the beetling cliffs
      that overlooked Pete's jerry-built contraption
      with people in aeries between
      hawks with eyes slitted
      in anticipation of water-kill
      while below in
      the copper blue lake
      a rowboat encircled the target zone in
      water mineralized to bear no life—
      barren, chaste womb
      unperturbed by penetralia
      free of scum, slime, or subterfuge
      for the innocent to take
      refuge—

            the exception being

        the copperheads that
        treaded listless with heat

the water alone lived
in its deep solicitude
receiving sun, moon, stars,
        time, nothing more
        before slinking back
        to the earth's den

Pete had grown gigantic
a giant who lived by his own rules
and rued no imagination besides
a fear of dwarves or dwarfing
diminution unto vapor

The special steel plank
welded in place by the Kerhonkson inspector
as the gaze went shoreside to
the agony of a catapult—
young red oak draw-knifed to
three-inch poles,
sanded and burnished with oil,
brass hardware for
a silken web around an iron cage
onto which fastened
a clapboard sign with the words:
DEATH TRAP

On the platform where they chained
him in the 'crusader's cross'
taught by the locking guilds,
the dark frock was a priest
there for last rites
as they lifted the bed for the women
whose wail keened the lake

◇ ◇ ◇

Nieuw Pfalz

Launched to 'Yankee Doodle,'
the sling hurled a dart at
the blinding sun, rock to fire, up, up, indecently
it shot, and when the cage
at its apogee paused,
as if suffering a change of heart,
it began to retract and double think
with an eructation of speed
to chasten thoughts of hope,
and it drove to invisibility
feet first into water—
arrested momentarily, some saw,
at ten feet of depth—
as if the intention met its impassibility
in a blinding recognition just
        long enough
        to deny
        simple human
        existence
before the acceleration down
to a bottomless silence

Only after an implausible wait
did men strip for the rescue

Pete who never finished
what there was on any subject
had gone hyperbaric
in order to converse with
the sinkhole